PRIVILEGE TO PRAY

International Standard Book Number: 9781677298747
Library of Congress Control Number: Txu 1-974-664

Copyright © 2015 by Denise Linder
Published by Denise Linder, Philadelphia Pa

Printed in the United States of America
Cover and Graphic Design Artist by: Amazon KDP Cover Creator

BIO

Denise Linder is the Author of several books; she is also an entrepreneur that operates a home base hand crafted costume jewelry business. She is a Minister of the Gospel of Jesus Christ. She is well known for her powerful revelation of scripture which can be seen sprawled across the pages of her books. Denise has one son, Reicco Linder Jr. and six beautiful grandchildren: five grandsons and one granddaughter.

Other books by Author

Issues and Answers

Adventures In Tithing

The Blood

The Art of Thanksgiving

Poverty

INTRODUCTION

This book is written to encourage readers to seek God on a daily basis. It's poetic flavor and normal everyday jargon will definitely grab the attention of those who really desire to increase their relationship with God. Along with this, it is written with busy people in mind. The prayers read or drive time are one minute or less of true down to earth heart grabbing golden nuggets. The prayers will allow you to stop, take a deep breath and earnestly honor God. It will remove all the guilt of not spending hours or being too busy to talk to God. The actual prayers will provoke you into time spent with God, whether it be five or ten minutes you will definitely be challenged after reading the prayer; and quite frankly feel totally refreshed!

DEDICATION

This book is dedicated to my best friend who taught me how to pray. He was very patient and kind to me. He encouraged me every step of the way. I didn't learn prayer from books or people, but he taught me through firsthand experience. I can never repay him for the knowledge he has imparted to me. The only way that I could reciprocate his loving mentorship is to pen his heart on the pages of this book. I pray that you would get to know my best friend the HOLY SPIRIT.

PRIVILEGE

TO

PRAY

GOOD MORNING WARRIORS!

You don't have to be
Brilliant As A rocket
Scientist. All You need is
To breathe the Breath of
God. His Breath penetrates
The second heaven, the
Playground of the activity
Of the demonic realm.
For your words of prayer
Carry the breath Of God.
They pierce the heart
Of darkness, they carve
A passageway for the
Glory of God to display
Himself. This occurs because
You dare summon him by
Your genuine hunger To
See him move on behalf
Of humanity. We are
Co-labours with Jesus Christ.

PRAY! PRAY! PRAY!

GOOD MORNING WARRIORS!

Gethsamane bares a repeat
Performance daily. For
Its lessons of praying
Through is astounding.
Jesus obtained mental
Strength inner fortitude to
Handle the world's sin
Problem. How much more
Shall we take a page out of
His life before we pick
Up our cross. It would be
Considerably easy to
Embrace the cross if we
Would pray through first.
Oh! The world would be
Ours for the taking.

PRAY! PRAY! PRAY!

GOOD MORNING WARRIORS!

Things are impossible
Because we deny God access
To them. We must without
Fail keep prayer pressure
On every impossibility.
For God declares I was
Found of them who sought
For me. Obstacles are
Opportunities for the
Miraculous. We must present
Every impossibility with
Brute force, for prayer
Pressure will produce an
Explosion of the fire and
Power of God.

PRAY! PRAY! PRAY

GOOD MORNING WARRIORS!

Conquerors attempt to
Defeat overwhelming odds
Against themselves. But
More than conquerors carry
The load of others to the
Throne room in Grand style.
With confused minds, and
Heavy hearts, with agitated
Fears, with broken and
Shattered lives and blood
Stain tears of love. More
Than conquerors press
Beyond measures of
Adversity to obtain
Victory for another.

PRAY! PRAY! PRAY!

GOOD MORNING WARRIORS!

Cheating the flesh of its
Passion to speak its purpose
Today will surely invite
A barrage of incredible
Mixed emotions: The
Fervor of mountain moving
Faith, the thrill of
Victory, The agony of
Silence, the chill of heavens
Presence. Also an intense
Shuddering of the will's
Strength to declare not
My will but thine be done.
This results in the
Manifestation of your
Heart's cry.

PRAY! PRAY! PRAY!

GOOD MORNING WARRIORS!

Strategists convene in
Order to map out plans
To accomplish certain tasks.
They prepare with great
Detail, fanfare, and hoopla.
They travel from near
And far hoping that the
Gathering of their minds
Labour will produce the
Desire results. Unfortunately
Failure's fruit proves
Efforts of time wasted.
But strategic prayer is
To pray daily with no
Fanfare. We have only
God's mind concerning
Every issue, always expecting
Solutions from our time
Spent with him. Now that's
The recipe for success!

PRAY! PRAY! PRAY!

GOOD MORNING WARRIORS!

The enemies' jugular is
Exposed and you have been
Commission to decapitate
It. Draw the sword of your
Tongue and sever every
Negative word against
You, yours, and others.
For the word is quick
And powerful. Formidable
Is your arsenal of faith
Filled words to achieve victory.

PRAY! PRAY! PRAY!

GOOD MORNING WARRIORS!

*It is an honor to
Communicate with God.
To be able at the flick
Of your Tongue, or the
Meditation of your heart,
Have an audience with his
Majesty. Carry every
Burden of your heart to
His chambers and leave
Them there. Rest and
Rekindle the flames of love
By intimate conversation
With him. He awaits your
Voice to be heard on high
To respond to your every
Request ardently.*

PRAY! PRAY! PRAY!

GOOD MORNING WARRIORS!

*The secret place is a
Place for warriors to
Congregate. There we
Retrieve the secrets of
The master to unlock the
Devices Of the enemy.
Entrance to the secret
Place is absolute surrender
And sacrifice of time.
Time is a priceless
Commodity. Wasted time
Is a tool of your adversary,
Designed to keep you from
The secret place. Monitor
Your time, for your enemy
Is more conscious of
Your time than you are.*

PRAY! PRAY! PRAY!

GOOD MORNING WARRIORS!

Pressing into the secret
Place irons out the
Wrinkles in our life.
Pressing's fruit yields
An ample supply of grace
To organize our cluttered
Lives. Its aim is to
Straighten out crooked
Places. Pressing beyond
Measure releases fire
Guaranteed to remove
The dross of pass failure,
Hopelessness and idleness.
It will reveal the work of
Grace done in secret.
Press in to see the
Transformation of the
New you. You'll be
Pleasantly surprised by
What awaits you.

PRAY! PRAY! PRAY!

GOOD MORNING WARRIORS!

Preparation is the
Master key for warfare.
Warfare is the master
Key For relinquishing
Of power. Power is the
Master key for advancement.
Advancement is the master
Key for success. Success
Is the Master Key for
Praise And worship of
Your god. Praise And
Worship Is the Master
Key to the releasing of
The Glory of God. Prayer
Sets the stage for it all.

PRAY! PRAY! PRAY!

GOOD MORNING WARRIORS!

You were endowed with
Weapons of mass destruction.
The weapon of pray postures
You on the throne, seating
You in heavenly places.
From this position your
Capable of peering into
The enemies'camp. Make
The enemy aware of your
Position, fight from the
Offensive position. Your
Position gives you the
Advantage, make the enemy
Hate to see you awake.

PRAY! PRAY! PRAY!

GOOD MORNING WARRIORS!

Prayer is the key that
Unlocks our heart. It
Exposes us to a life of
The supernatural. It
Awakens us from the
Dull dreary carnal wooing's
Of the flesh. It eclipses
A soul over burden with
Drudgery from passionless
Fellowship. In his
Presence is Fullness of
Joy. Prayer ignites
Our souls, lights our
Path and brings clarity
Of vision. It processes
And propels us into purpose
Why would you not pray?

PRAY! PRAY! PRAY!

GOOD MORNING WARRIORS!

There are times and
Seasons when revenge is
Placed in your hands to be
Utilized. Seasons of intense
Prayer and fasting would
Be one of those. Take a
Sit down, reflect on your
Arch enemies tactics to
Annihilate you. Is it a
Time to kill or a time to
Speak. A time to hate
And a time to war. Kill
Every demonic influence
By speaking the word. Hate
Everything he has ever
Done to you and go to war
For vengeance is yours.

PRAY! PRAY! PRAY!

GOOD MORNING WARRIORS!

We have been summoned
To be trailblazers. To
Pioneer through intercession
Paths of liberty. For the
Liberation of your family
And friends are his
Passion's plea. For your
Prayer will show them the
Path. But your love
Will escort them down the
Paths of least resistant
Forge on my bride, my
Beloveds pursue, overtake
And embrace the momentum
Of the pursuit.

PRAY! PRAY! PRAY!

GOOD MORNING WARRIORS!

Laboring in prayer is
A work of grace which
Has a twofold purpose.
First, prayer brings you
Under direct scrutiny of
The cleansing fire of God
It is quite challenging
And courageous for us to
Be committed to prayer
For the express purpose
Of dealing with ourselves.
Secondly, it's purpose
Is to stay and pray long
Enough so the first
Purpose can be
Accomplished. Cry out to
God that you may be
Meat for the master's use.

PRAY! PRAY! PRAY!

GOOD MORNING WARRIORS!

Prayerlessness is equal
To being incarcerated,
Lock down under the
Tyranny of the flesh.
Your every move is
Dictated by its impulses.
It Systematically
Rehabilitates its former
Years of a life full of
Doubt and despair. But
Be encouraged God still
Opens prison doors. A
Open mouth is the key.
Release yourself from
Prison and get back into
Path of life. For new
Opportunities are searching
You out.

PRAY! PRAY! PRAY!

GOOD MORNING WARRIORS!

Prayer builds character,
Even when your character
At times displays itself
Unseemingly. Just the mere
Fact that you positioned
Yourself before his throne,
Demonstrates your desire
For Transformation. The
Place of Prayer, is a
Place of selflessness. In
This place, the Master's
Character continues to
Chisel away at our heart,
Conforming us into his
Divine nature.

PRAY! PRAY! PRAY!

GOOD MORNING WARRIORS!

*Spiritual gifts and ministry
Concerns, and things we have
Scheduled to busy ourselves
Does not preempt our
Responsibility to commune with
The lord. Jesus consistently
Broke away from the masses
For the purpose of prayer.
Prayer was factored in his 24
Hour period of life. He lived a
Prayer driven life. Without
Consistent prayer you will
Experience pride's syndrome.
Your insight, your strength,
Your ambition. Reach for him
Today, lay down your reputation,
Your greatness and have a
Little talk with Jesus.*

PRAY! PRAY! PRAY!

GOOD MORNING WARRIORS!

Without prayer your
Blinded to stagnation's
Deception. You will
Wallow in a faded vision
With hindsight as your
Compass. Prayer is necessary
To revive your expectancy,
To reach beyond the pass
Experiences of faded
Glory. Prayer schedules
A show down of new
Adventures and refreshes
The promises of God. Prayer
Invokes renewed life
And strength of heart.
So, build upon your
Renewed fellowship and
Watch stagnation's fruit flee.

PRAY! PRAY! PRAY!

GOOD MORNING WARRIORS!

*Prayer leaves an indelible
Mark on those to whom we
Direct it. Your words
Will wrestle and harass
The conscience of your
Targets. Prayer opens
Prison doors of pain,
Sickness, poverty, calamities
And shame. It is the
Most powerful weapon in
Existence. But the least
Utilized by its predecessors.
Praying is the proof of
Your Reliance on God.
Prayer brings God great
Glory. The battle for your
Words are of utmost
Importance, Use them wisely.*

PRAY! PRAY! PRAY!

GOOD MORNING WARRIORS!

*Prayer is heaven's
Currency. Prayer's
Purchasing power is
Unlimited. Prayer provides
Us debt relief from sin's
Expense. The returns on
Prayer is Priceless. It
Is the number one cost
Effective investment we
Should partake in. It
Yields heaven's glory.
Prayer is a sure thing
The master is searching
For interested investors
That will go all in. Your
Eternal benefits will
Increase the more. Prayer
Reaps heaven's dividends
Forever more.*

PRAY! PRAY! PRAY!

GOOD MORNING WARRIORS!

What amazes you about our
Father? Is it that he forgives
Our sins. Or that he has
Rescued our children, maybe
Your life has been powerfully
Blessed. I'm amazed
That He always wants to talk
With us no matter what we do.
I am amazed that he wants to
Share his kingdom with us. I'm
Amazed with his patience with
Us. I'm amazed that he wants us.
I'm Amazed that he said whatsoever
Thing you desire when you pray
Believe that you receive it and
You will have it. I'm amazed
That he's so amazing

PRAY! PRAY! PRAY

GOOD MORNING WARRIORS!

*God is interested in heaven
On earth. To achieve his
Purposes, we need to submit
To the clarion call to pray.
For the sound of war has
Been heralded, the troops
Must assemble for battle.
Prayer's call has penetrated
The earth's stratosphere.
The earth is preparing to
Host his Glory. Gird up
Your mind, adorn yourselves
With your royal battle attire.
Let's advance with the force
Of faith to retrieve our
King's kingdom agenda for
Whom his soul travailed.*

PRAY! PRAY! PRAY!

GOOD MORNING WARRIORS!

*If the odds are stacked
Against you, than you have
The upper hand. Prayer
Levels the playing field
Where victory is assured.
Praying In faith's field
Disarms doubt and ruffles
The feathers of fear. It
Transports a superior mind
Grounded in grace. The
Heart prays without
Ceasing when adversity
Stands erect, it agrees
With the LORD who has
The final call. So, press
On, take the field of
Prayer to receive your
Winners crown.*

PRAY! PRAY! PRAY!

GOOD MORNING WARRIORS!

*A person of prayer will always
Have the king's scepter
Extended towards them, for
They have chosen to be an
Extension of him. For they press
In daily Expecting pleasant
Conversation. They want what
He wants, so they wait and wait
And wait. Hunger is their
Driving force, so waiting isn't
Tiresome, it isn't boring it's
Their hearts delight. Faith
Makes them trust that he'll
Speak, so insight becomes their
Foresight. God honors their
Presence and empties himself on
Them. Oh! The glory of his presence.*

PRAY! PRAY! PRAY!

GOOD MORNING WARRIORS!

*Seek ye first the kingdom
Of God literally means
To seek the King. Search
For him with all your
Heart. A rendezvous is
Sometime permissible, but
For lasting results requires
A deeper commitment to
Seeking. Launch Out into
The deep, lose yourself in
The depths of him. Allow
Yourself to become intimately
Acquainted with the fullness
Of his love. For he wishes
With all his heart that
You may become fond of him.*

PRAY! PRAY! PRAY!

GOOD MORNING WARRIORS!

The measure of one's love
Is seen in the experience
It's willing to partake of.
Are you willing to share
The burden of intercession
With Jesus? To travail and
Prevail threw Seasons of love.
To battle the Forces of nature
The self-life with it's never
Ending wooing's. To pray
For the liberation of a
Soul. To be uncompromising
In prayer until victory
Shouts her voice, it is
Finish. And love has
Won out. Prayer finishes
What the cross started.

PRAY! PRAY! PRAY!

GOOD MORNING WARRIORS!

Who do you spend all your
Time with. Is your time
Spent in a love affair
With the past. Is it
Spent daydreaming in
False grandeur. Is it
Spent jesting and carousing?
Is it spent in two 9 to 5's?
Wise warriors can never
Get enough of meditating
On his goodness. Stolen
Moments are fine, but
Quality time with him is
Divine. How much are you
Willing to spend just to be
With him? When greatness
Calls will you have any time
Left for him.

PRAY! PRAY! PRAY!

GOOD MORNING WARRIORS!

Jesus really believes his
Children would benefit
Most if they would become
Regimented in prayer.
What do you believe? Jesus
Really believes that time
Spent with him in prayer
Deepens your relationship
With him? What do you
Believe? Jesus really believes
That prayer is the first
Solution to problem solving.
What do you believe? Jesus
Really believes that prayer
Changes things supernaturally.
What do you believe? Hmmm,
If you're not praying, I wonder
What you believe?

PRAY! PRAY! PRAY!

GOOD MORNING WARRIORS!

Time is of the essence.
Time spent with him has
No Equal or rival. For
He created time while
Encased in eternity. If
Your time is monopolized
In time in idleness of
Heart, then the
Supernatural is waning.
Your desires have become
Stagnated in times
Atmosphere. Prayers key
Is the go between to
Unlock eternity in the earth.
Prayer management is
Essential to eternities
Unfolding grace.

PRAY! PRAY! PRAY!

GOOD MORNING WARRIORS!

Here's a love letter for God's
Warriors. How can I express
My love any more than I have
Thus far, reveal to me you're
Deepest plea. For I yearn
For the closeness of your breath
To partake of its loving caress.
Your words arouse my core, your
Imploring's shalt not be ignored.
Day after day I embrace your
Hearts cry. You're so necessary
To me, oh so necessary to me as
Honey is to bees. Come to me my
Beloved, and speak sweet whispers
Of love, signed the lover of
Your soul.

PRAY! PRAY! PRAY!

GOOD MORNING WARRIORS!

Prayer is a weapon against
Fleshly tendencies. It
Deadens it's passions by
Placing it in a coma.
Subconsciously it is aware
Of its surroundings, but
Has been Stripped of its
Strength to Perform.
Prayer has a profound
Effect on the norms of
Carnality. It builds
Spiritual power, it moves in
A circle of its own. Prayer
Surrounds your mind with
The supernatural, there
The natural is ignored.
Prayer crucifies the flesh
Again and again and again.

PRAY! PRAY! PRAY!

GOOD MORNING WARRIORS!

*Prayer is like a game of
Chess. Every movement is
Strategic, the king and
Queen dominates all other
Players. The queen which
Is equal to the bride of
Christ is the most
Powerful of all. She can
Go anywhere and do any
Thing. For her advantages
In her domain are unlimited.
She moves in kingdom faith
Understanding her position.
For she lives to defeat the
Deceptive practices of all
Opposition. How about you? Is
Your prayer life strategic.
Do you have confidence in
Your seated position of
Prayer?*

PRAY! PRAY! PRAY

GOOD MORNING WARRIORS!

*Making the decision to pray
Consistently will bring great
Inner conflict. Outward
Opposition is the least of your
Concerns, especially when your
Mind is made up to pray. When
Prayer becomes your occupation,
Your profession, your lifeline,
Then and only then will it
Become a force of habit.
Fellowshipping with the Holy
Spirit will bring promotion,
Increase and productivity in
Your life. For his profession
Is to make you successful in all
That you do, to bring glory to
The father. Wanted! Prayer
Warriors, signed up today.*

PRAY! PRAY! PRAY!

GOOD MORNING WARRIORS!

Prayer invites the master's
Touch in every situation.
When his presence graces
The stage, men's minds are
Changed. For they have been
Struck by loves embrace.
Prayer alleviates careless
Whispers that resonate
Loudly in our hearts. It
Assures us of his abiding
Presence. Prayer is a
Fortress that stands alone.
To commune with the master
Is the greatest compliment
Of our day. Thank you
Father for desiring
Conversation with me. Let
Me respond back in kind.

PRAY! PRAY! PRAY!

GOOD MORNING WARRIORS!

Prayer is like a compass.
It will show you exactly
Where you're are. Prayer
Will change the direction
Of your life within a
Instance shift. Prayer
Will guide you through
Wildernesses and desert
Places. It's favorite
Direction is due north
Which always causes
Movement upward. If you
Seem to have loss your
Way and unsure of the
Path to take. Let prayer
Be your compass for it's
Leading will always lead
To the master's place.

PRAY! PRAY! PRAY!

GOOD MORNING WARRIORS!

Prayer builds memorials.
Its root is deeply
Lodged at heaven's door.
Prayer opens the gate
Welcoming you to feast
In his presence. Prayer
Mobilizes angelic
Enforcements forming
Passageways to his
Throne. Before a breath
Escapes your lips your
Request is met with
Haste. Diligently carve
Until your memorial has
A face formed
Fashioned by consistent
Prayer.

PRAY! PRAY! PRAY!

GOOD MORNING WARRIORS!

Scripture declares that I
Might know him in the power
Of his resurrection and the
Fellowship of his suffering
Prayer is not exempted in
This text. Praying to the
Father daily gave him courage to
Carry out the father's purpose
In Gethsamane, he prayed not
My will, but thine be done
Supernatural courage and
Strength of mind was released
In this prayer. He could now
Not be stopped, making all
Things possible to him. It's the
Same for you and me. We can
Achieve courageous things for
God if we pray.

PRAY! PRAY! PRAY!

GOOD MORNING WARRIORS!

*Have you got the going to
Church working in the
Kingdom blues? Prayer will
Bring you back to your first
Love. Everything else is a
 Affair of the heart designed
To woo you away from him.
Gathering at the hour of
Prayer is a sure-fire way to
Guard against apathy. The
Prayer gathering is a place
Of renewal of mind and vision.
Gathering in the chosen place
Refreshes the soul and spirit,
It makes ready purposes to
Soar. It builds relationships
It teaches, trains, and mentors
Us the more. It brings strength
To discouraged hearts, this
Will keep us coming back
To the house of prayer.*

PRAY! PRAY! PRAY!

GOOD MORNING WARRIORS!

*Daily prayer is the key to
Breakthrough. It will break
Stubborn tendencies of the
Flesh. It will break wrong
Thought patterns. Prayer seeks
Out hidden agendas of the
Heart. It reveals our true
Motives. Scripture declares
The heart is deceitful and
Desperately wicked. No one knows
Our hearts like God. We're
Not sure of the things resident
Within it if prayer is lacking.
Daily visits to Doctor Jesus
Are necessary. This will keep
Our hearts free from becoming
Harden from trials, persecution,
And the works of the flesh.
Keep your appointments.*

PRAY! PRAY! PRAY!

GOOD MORNING WARRIORS!

Prayer is the greatest
Communicating system ever
Known to man in all generations.
Its capabilities extend through
Out the entire universe. When
Put into motion it creates havoc
In the kingdom of darkness.
Nothing is out of the reach of
Its clutches. Prayer starts
Revolutions, revolts, and revivals.
Prayer loose's angelic military
Might, and causes cease fires in
Human lives. It commands the
Elements. It gives you a direct
Line to your commander in
Chief. With such a powerful tool
At our disposal we can do wonders.

PRAY! PRAY! PRAY!

GOOD MORNING WARRIORS!

*Prayer should not be a mere
Passing thought, second in
Nature to our busyness.
Prayer balances the
Believer's life based
Upon its place of importance.
A thousand pounds of life's
Pressure versus a breathe of
Prayer is equal in weight.
For prayer will balance
Enormous weights. For
It is the heavyweight champ
That champions your world.
For Champions do daily
The necessary requirements
To be a champ. Allow prayer
To instruct you in the ways
Of becoming a champion
Of your world.*

PRAY! PRAY! PRAY!

GOOD MORNING WARRIORS!

The art of intercession
Is lodged in the depths
Of your spirit. The power
Of release is in your
Tongue. Determine to
Unleash this reservoir
In you. Just do it! When
Discouraged, just do it!
In confusion, just do it!
When persecuted, just
Do it! On the mountain
Top, just do it! In the
Valley, just do it! In
Every time and season,
Just do it! Just doing it!
Is the art of intercession!

PRAY! PRAY! PRAY!

GOOD MORNING WARRIORS!

Prayer sets the stage for an
Adventurous life. Prayer
Allows you to see farther
Then you ever believed you
Could. The complexity of prayer
Is astounding. It travels on the
Circuits of heaven and earth to
Impact its purpose. It's sounds
Penetrates men hearts. It
Paralyzes the enemy and moves
The hand of God. It's success
Motivates you to continue in its
Wonders. There's nowhere in
The entire world that can escape
The rippling effect of prayer.
If they close our mouths, our
Hearts will battle on, there is no
Defense to prayer, it's invincible.

PRAY! PRAY! PRAY!

GOOD MORNING WARRIORS!

Prayer is like a diamond
Of great price. A diamond
Is forever, prayer will
Change your life forever.
The fashioning of you
Is done in the dark places.
Prayer will illuminate
Your pathway, it will
Lead you through the
Many facets of life.
Prayer has an assignment.
Prayer is designed to make
Sure you stand when you
Don't understand the
Why, when, and how of the
Journey. Prayer is
Brilliance on display in
The face of adversarial
Forces. Shine saints shine.

PRAY! PRAY! PRAY!

GOOD MORNING WARRIORS!

We are admonished by God
To leave an inheritance
To our children's children.
What legacy have we set
Before them. Are they
Eyewitnesses of the practice
Of prayer in our homes?
Is the family altar in
Existence or extinct?
Habitual prayer builds
Its own lasting legacy
If witnessed by our
Children. It's caught and
Taught. It's show and tell.
The legacy of prayer is
The foundation for
Generational success
Continually.

PRAY! PRAY! PRAY!

GOOD MORNING WARRIORS!

*Warriors fight for the
Honour of the King. They
Masterfully prepare to do
Battle at a moment's notice.
The king's agenda takes
Precedence over everything.
The business of prayer is the
The warriors weapon. Each
Warrior is highly skilled and
Gracious in the how to of
Combat they pray knowing
They have the victory. In
Confidence the sword of
Prayer is wielded. Warriors
Gladly expend themselves to
Please the king. Only
Eternity will reveal the
Prayer warriors rewards.*

PRAY! PRAY! PRAY!

GOOD MORNING WARRIORS!

Prayer is equal to a thermostat
You set its controls. Energy
Efficient is the perfect module.
Prayer is efficient for every
Climatic shift that arises
With hostile intent. It will
Maintain the condition of
Your heart amid fiery trials.
Prayer increases faith when the
Cold calculation of adversarial
Fits of carnality come knocking.
Prayer's energy will stable the
Mind from invading pressures
Attempting to adjust your faith
Focus. Prayer will empower the
Faith fight. It will hand you
The victory. Prayer will cause
The flesh to throw in the towel.

PRAY! PRAY! PRAY!

GOOD MORNING WARRIORS!

Your prayers are a fragrance
Unto God. The aroma is so
Dear to him, that he commissioned
Angels to bottle them in vials.
Your prayers are precious and
Protected by angelic forces. the
Odour of prayer is so powerful
That it is the answer to the
Stench of sin. Every breath
That escapes Your lips is sweet to
The Saviour. It builds fortresses
Guarding the life of humanity.
Prayer reeks of victory
Prayer captures the heart of
God. It's the incense of the
The father's dwelling place.
Prayers fragrance attracts the
Supernatural on your behalf.

PRAY! PRAY! PRAY!

GOOD MORNING WARRIORS!

The fastest way to victory is
To pray your way through. For
Some the journey has been long
And hard fought. Lulls and
Lack of prayer delays the process
Of being processed. Prayer
Gears should be on cruise
Control. Every God giving rest
Stop fills you with new oil.
Prayer helps you to bypass
Hazardous pit stops and
Pitfalls. Prayers atlas is as a
Shining path leading you down
The King's highway. If we
Follow his direction we'll
Arrive at our destination on time.
Allow the vehicle of prayer to
Escort you through the processes
Of life.

PRAY! PRAY! PRAY!

GOOD MORNING WARRIORS!

*Prayer brings the justice of God
In all matters of the kingdom.
Prayer will prosecute the
Persecutors of injustice. Prayer
Will defend the rights of his
People. Prayer alone is judge
And jury. Prayer is due process
In action. Prayer is the
Executing of divine retribution
Against all unfair practices.
Prayer's consultation fee is free.
Prayer brings down the angelic
Jurisdictional weight of heavens
Law firm. Prayer's argument
Will Always result in case
Dismissed. Allow prayer to
Be your advocate, the odds
Are in your favor.*

PRAY! PRAY! PRAY!

GOOD MORNING WARRIORS!

Faith's ability to perform
Is seen in the steadfastness
Of our prayer lives. Prayer
Is the place of vision.
It focuses its sight on the
Realm of impossibilities.
Prayer wages war for the
Destiny of a thing until it
Has been safely secured.
Praying in faith demonstrates
Superior allegiance to our
Master's word. Prayer
Prevents our wombs from
Miscarrying his purpose.
It assures the seed's stability
To reach full term. Prayer
Is necessary to birth your
Precious promises.

PRAY! PRAY! PRAY!

GOOD MORNING WARRIORS!

*Prayer settles the
Schizophrenic mind, amid
The many conversations
Playing at will. Unleashing
Tongues of fire will
Arrest opposing thoughts.
Prayer's energy placates the
Sub-conscious. Prayer is
The guarding force of your
Mind. Prayer is a must and
Must be stationed to capture
Incoming ideas not affiliated
With your assignment.
Praying in peace time is just
As vital as praying in times
Of war for continued success.
Prayer keeps your mind in
Perfect peace.*

PRAY! PRAY! PRAY!

GOOD MORNING WARRIORS!

Prayer has resurrection
Power. It is most renown
For its ability to renew,
Realign, revamp, restore,
Reinvigorate, recapture,
Reinstate, remobilize, the
Whole of you. The prayer
Of the righteous availeth
Much. The power of recovery
Has it's root in prayer.
Failure has exposed us to
The recovery power of prayer.
It brakes the cycle of loss
If entered into humbly.
Prayer's agenda is so vast
That a lifetime is to short
A time to grasp it's
Magnificence. Prayer is a
Confidence builder if we
Would believe in the recovery
Power of it.

PRAY! PRAY! PRAY!

GOOD MORNING WARRIORS!

*Prayer is a pleasure
Principle. It pleases the
Father. God created words
As his vehicle of
Communication. The word
Then decided to shape himself
In humanities attire.
Upon his ascension the word's
Abilities was willed to us.
He expects us to call those
Things that be not as though
They are. He gave prayer as
A directive of commanded
Force. Prayer is a direct
Order to be obeyed. Elements
Are to obey, the demonic
World is to obey. Even God
Obeys the prayer of the
Humble. We must and should
Obey God's command to.*

PRAY! PRAY! PRAY!

GOOD MORNING WARRIORS!

The power of prayer has never
Been considered ancient or
Obsolete. For it is the only
Course of action that has
Transcended with the changing
Of times. There is no ingenuity
To prayer, it's ingenious. The
Infrastructure of prayer is
Impenetrable. It has been hands
Down the single most utilized and
Successful principle of all time.
Its effectiveness have proven to
Be invaluable by mankind in every
Generation. Perfection needs not
To be tampered with. We will
Benefit most if we extend it's
Legacy to the coming generations.

PRAY! PRAY! PRAY!

GOOD MORNING WARRIORS!

_Prayer is the language of
Love. Synergy prayer is
Harmony in heaven. Prayer
Orchestrates the release of
Grace in abundance. Every
Prayer chord brings love
Struck victors to the cross
Of Calvary. Prayer is highly
Dramatic in nature. Tongues
Of fire alone alerts the dark-
Ness of its soon coming
Demise. Praying for your
Enemies is the greatest
Illustration of love, coals of
Fire are coals of love. Love
Languishing affects continues
Fueled by prayer._

PRAY! PRAY! PRAY!

GOOD MORNING WARRIORS!

*Prayer is the constitution of
The believer. It regulates and
Legislates the BRANCH's
Government. Prayer exacts
Illegal proposals in high places.
It is the amending power of the
Subconscious of man. The
Judicial strength of a kingdom
Is enforced in prayer. Prayer
Is a noble cause, and the signet
Of nobility. It is one of the
Highest honors to be knighted
With. It is our responsibility
To release our constitution in
A three-dimensional world to
Supersede the existing
Government of darkness.*

PRAY! PRAY! PRAY!

GOOD MORNING WARRIORS!

*Prayer and trust go hand in
Hand. The two are inseparable,
Praying demonstrates our
Reliance upon God.
Prayerlessness leaves the spirit
Hungry and willing to devour
Religious jargon. This
Disadvantages the soul making
It susceptible to countless
Physical indulgences. Prayer
Must be central to the believers
Life. It governs the inward and
Outward men. Prayer must not
Become traditional repetitions,
But an aura of glowing embers
Powered by faith filled words.*

PRAY! PRAY! PRAY!

GOOD MORNING WARRIORS!

Intercessory prayer is a tool
That shatters strongholds. It
Calls for great feats of will
Power and strength. It's the
Ultimate battle with the flesh.
The flesh has many devices to
Challenge intercessory prayer.
It favors the weapon of boredom.
But cunning intercessors
Invite spells of boredom. We
Prepare in advance to stay the
Course, realizing the necessity
Of overcoming boredom is the
Breaking point of birthing a
Intercessory ministry. The
Daily chore of boredom is
Leading the way to victory.

PRAY! PRAY! PRAY!

GOOD MORNING WARRIORS!

*Prayer sets the atmosphere
For God's glory to be released.
The nature of prayer is a
Panacea that has no rival in
Existence. The battle for
Supremacy is fought in the
Trenches of prayer. Prayer
Causes the heart of God to
Reign. Prayer expands your
Belief system. It welcomes all
impossible situational ethics
To defeat it's cause. For
It thrives in the face of
Dubious assaults. Tenacious
Prayer will outlast temptations
Compromise. Prayer makes you
More than a Conqueror.*

PRAY! PRAY! PRAY!

GOOD MORNING WARRIORS!

To cease praying is to place
Your life in neutral. We'll
Have allusions of progress
But we're only marking time.
The process to movement
Again is to grab a hold of
The altar, and to pray on
Purpose. You must discipline
Yourself when it comes to
Prayer. Praying will
Challenge your flesh, it will
Take every ounce of might
To stay the course. Pressing
Into prayer will ignite the
Soul. Your passion will burst
Through, and your direction
Will be clear. Causing you
To mount up with wings of
An eagle and to run your race
Effortlessly and courageously.

PRAY! PRAY! PRAY!

GOOD MORNING WARRIORS!

Prayer is discreet but
Plainly unique. It's claim
To fame is found in the many
Infallible proofs of changed
Lives. Praying sets men up
For success, it transforms
The minds of men. Mere men
Become supermen when they
Turn their hearts to God in
Prayer. Incorporating daily
Prayer in your life turns the
Odds swiftly in your favor.
The compilation of miracles
Is a testament to the greatness
Of this practice. Prayer has
Penned the history of man.

PRAY! PRAY! PRAY!

GOOD MORNING WARRIORS!

*Prayer is practiced in all
Cultures. It is the currency
Or medium of exchange for
Most who invest in it. But for
Those who trust in Jesus,
Prayer is the umbilical cord
Of life. It is the language
Of the kingdom, the strength
Of our culture. The capital
Of our economy, the constitution
Of our government. The wealth
Of our health system. The
Commander of our military
Might. The standard for wisdom
And excellent. And the reason
We live to intercede on behalf
Of cult like cultures who spew
Words of peril to deceive.*

PRAY! PRAY! PRAY!

GOOD MORNING WARRIORS!

*Prayer, like a surround sound
System reverberates until
Impact on a global scale is
Felt. Intercessory prayer
Travels in wave after wave
After wave, overwhelming
Every obstacle in its path.
The pioneering accuracy of
Intercessory prayer renders
It's opposition helpless. The
Sheer magnitude of it's
Tsunami like affect implodes
Enemy sieges. The prayer of
Faith is your surround sound
System willed to you for
Consistent use. Verbalize,
Energize, monopolize, your
World for spiritual impact.*

PRAY! PRAY! PRAY!

GOOD MORNING WARRIORS!

Prayer forms a cyclone of
Power. It is counterproductive
To the works of the flesh and
Of darkness. Prayer protects
The flourishing of God's
Purposes. The discerning
Component of prayer detects
The slightest atmospheric
Disturbances. Prayer defines
It's objectives then surge's forth
To victory. Every child of God
Is a warrior endowed with
Inalienable rights. The right to
Execute heaven's law and order.
The right to overthrow criminal
Minds. We by praying invite
The visibility of the invisible
To show himself strong on our
Behalf.

PRAY! PRAY! PRAY!

<u>*GOOD MORNING WARRIORS!*</u>

*Prayer is equal to a pearl of
Great price. The beauty of
Prayer is engulfed in intrigue.
The friction it embraces to
Bring value and luster to a
Life is privy to those who value
The secret place. To pray is
To pay the price for greatness.
Praying while foreign irritants
Invade your space sets the bar
High for perseverance's fruit.
Prayer's results mystifies it's
Foes as it witness beauty emerge
From the beast. My prayer has
Provoked my foes to adorn me
Ever so graciously, until the
Fashioning of me is priceless.*

<u>*PRAY! PRAY! PRAY!*</u>

GOOD MORNING WARRIORS!

To pray is to stay abreast
Of spiritual matter and
Current events. Prayer
Keeps your discernment
Sharp and your heart
Ablaze with truth. It
Commands the recognition
Due it by the exploits it has
Accomplished. The successful
Warriors have prayer as a
Lifestyle, a profession, and a
Leisure all in one. The
Pleasure prayer brings can
Only be summoned up by the
Many who have experienced
It's tangible freedoms.
Prayer is the real deal.

PRAY! PRAY! PRAY!

GOOD MORNING WARRIORS!

*Prayer extends the health of the
Believer. The dynamics of prayer
Are endless. Praying the word
Over yourself brings health and
Wholeness. The word of God is the
Greatest self-help book of all time
It is extremely important that we
Help our self to it. It has many
Tips on friendships, money, sex,
Marriage, singles, religion,
Politics, children, global economics,
Leadership, education, military,
Government, law and order, health,
Agriculture, food, alcohol. It is a
Must for all humanity. Pray for it's
Continuance to further the cause
Of righteousness.*

PRAY! PRAY! PRAY!

GOOD MORNING WARRIORS!

Prayer brings light to every
Dark situation. Prayer travels
Faster than the speed of
Light. Praying the word gives
Definition and expels Com-
Placency. Prayers accuracy
Promotes faith and rejects the
Notion of traditional moaning
And groaning. The light
Of God's word shines
Brightest amid trials and fears.
It leads us threw the shadow
Of darkness. It exposes every
Secret in men hearts.
Nothing is held from the
Light of God, for light and
Dark both are equal in his
Sight.

PRAY! PRAY! PRAY!

GOOD MORNING WARRIORS!

Mountain moving faith is
Increased in strategic prayer.
Not my will but thou be done, are
The greatest words ever spoken.
It finished the revolution of
Mankind. Mountains crumbled
Under the weight of that prayer.
The greatest mountain ever to
Exist was the sin sick soul of
Mankind. Jesus in one sentence
Pulverized sin's core. Every
Stripe ratified and opened
Redemptions door. Sins
Mountain, the utopias mount upon
Which we stand, keeps us praying
In Faith until every man
Receives the master's plan of
Grace.

PRAY! PRAY! PRAY!

GOOD MORNING WARRIORS!

Prayer causes you to mount
Up with wings as an eagle.
Prayer thrust you from earth
To heaven in a moments
Notice. Prayer's sight sees
In the distant future, secures
The plan of battle and prepares
Accordingly. Prayer's mental
Acuity issues from God's war
Room assuring the triumph of
The conflict. The penetrating
Pupils of prayer advances
With extreme aggression both
Day and night. It captures
The purposes for which the
Pursuit was deemed necessary.
From the spectacular visions
From heaven.

PRAY! PRAY! PRAY!

GOOD MORNING WARRIORS!

Prayer gives you access to the
Central intelligence agency of
The kingdom. Prayer
Circumvents principalities
Premeditated plans. The generals
Of prayer contrive precisely
Their downfall. God is
Always calling his warriors
To the battlefield of the
Mind. It's the primary place
Of victory before the spiritual
Conflict begins. Preparation is
Keeping your prayer life
Intact. The warrior's heart
Stay's alert and is groomed
For duty 24/7.

PRAY! PRAY! PRAY!

GOOD MORNING WARRIORS!

*Prayer is a performance in
Theatrics. The riveted audience
Of eternity stands aloof hanging
On your every word. Prayer
Brings to pass the script of
God in the drama of human life.
Praying is the greatest role
You'll ever perform in your
Entire life. There will never
Be a time when a script or a
Role is not available. Eternity
Is depending upon your
Availability. You'll have
Opportunity after opportunity
To play Jesus as the great
Intercessor. Prayer is them
Drama of heaven's reality
On life's stage.*

PRAY! PRAY! PRAY!

GOOD MORNING WARRIORS!

Prayer is truly passion on
Display. It is at times quite
Dramatic. It can be serenely
Entered into. It could be of
Dignified eloquence. Or may
Be violent to say the least at
Times. Your prayer personality
Oozes your passion. The
Master revels in the sounds
And movements of the real
You. Real prayer is to do you
When fellowshipping with him.
Every part of you is an arsenal
To be reckoned with. No
Other style of prayer is as
Grand, gracious, or tenacious.
Once you have poised yourself
For battle. Represent, do you.

PRAY! PRAY! PRAY!

GOOD MORNING WARRIORS!

*Prayer is vital to your belief
System. It keeps the heart
Primed and full of faith.
Prayer severs ties with the
World of doubt and unbelief.
To pray is to take daily
Journeys to the invisible
World, retrieve little by
Little the solutions sought
For until the whole of it is
In your possession. Prayer
Keeps faith vibrant and
Moving. Prayer is molding
The inner man, fashioning
Him into a gladiator. We
Were born for faith fights,
It's been willed to us in his
Last will and testament. Get
Up, stay up, are you ready
To rumble.*

PRAY! PRAY! PRAY!

GOOD MORNING WARRIORS!

*Prayer is the embryonic stage
For a life full of miracles.
Prayer prepares you as a vessel
Of choice. A thoroughly
Committed life to prayer
Invokes the tangible presence
Of God. He hangs off your
Every word and thought. He
Finds it hard to resist your
Presence. Praying alone has
Qualified you without fore-
Thought to be his friend, he
Values friendship above all.
In choosing to pray you have
Opted for a life of sacrifice.
This can only equal in part to
The feat of one of Christ's great
Sacrifices, living to make
Intercession. Prayer is not
For wimps it's for warriors.*

PRAY! PRAY! PRAY!

GOOD MORNING WARRIORS!

Nothing is more exciting then
The pursuit of something.
Prayer produces zealousness.
A momentum that refuses to
Exercise the thoughts of
Commonality. Prayer mounts
Itself with a superior mind set
Fortified from its command
Center's agenda. It sees
Beyond the present obstacle's
Deceit. The discerning
Qualities of prayer takes
Center's stage. It calls a spade
A spade. Retreat has not been
Wired into its central
Processing unit. Prayer
Relishes the pursuit of
Impossibilities, for it is
The arena of its greatest
Achievements and the
Honored life.

PRAY! PRAY! PRAY!

GOOD MORNING WARRIORS!

*God invites us to invite him into
The affairs of the world. Prayer
Is the hallmark of the believer.
Prayer opens the door to the
Global conscious. God responded
To your prayer's RSVP before the
Words escaped your lips. He
Accepts with intentions of being
The light and life of the
Party. He came bearing the gifts
Of grace, righteousness, and
Faith. He absolutely swells at
The thought of you inviting him
To be a part of destroying the
Works of the enemy. Allow your
Tongue to be the pen of a ready
Writer. He awaits the invite
With eager anticipation.*

PRAY! PRAY! PRAY!

GOOD MORNING WARRIORS!

Diligence and prayer are a
Unbeatable tandem. Diligence is
A necessity to bring prayer
To its fullest potential outcome.
Diligence is the root core of
Prayer. Without diligence the
Enemy of instability will
Enter the picture uninvited,
Bringing along with it it's
Confederate friends of
Lukewarmness, procrastination,
And sluggishness. Due diligence
Must be incorporated to stymie
The opposition's onslaught of
These. The rewards of diligence
In prayer is a lavish system of
Unending victories awaiting your
Arrival at the finish line.

PRAY! PRAY! PRAY!

GOOD MORNING WARRIORS!

*Prayer should be an occupational
Hazard. It's the most dangerous
Of all jobs under heaven. It's
Job description is to start fires,
To trespass areas off limits to
Humans, prayer is a bully and a
Vigilante, it's always hostile.
Prayer creates scandals exposing
Dirt. Prayer is the believers
Drug of choice. We should make
Sure we get high on a daily
Basis. Prayer fights until
Blood prevails. The job of
Prayer is so awesome and
Powerful so necessary to match
Wits legally to eradicate
Evil. What a job.*

PRAY! PRAY! PRAY!

GOOD MORNING WARRIORS!

*Right praying is a thing of
Beauty. It takes the evils of
Life and society and
Restructures it from the inside
Out. Prayer has a jagged edge
Effect. Everything it touches
Is subject to change. Prayer
Begins the tedious task of
First attacking dangerous
Ideologies. Prayer launches
Truth to the con's core,
Dismissing it, leaving behind
Truths fragrance. Prayer's
Aroma lingers assuring the
Masterpiece materializes until
The external replicates the
Deposits of truth left behind.*

PRAY! PRAY! PRAY!

GOOD MORNING WARRIORS!

*Prayer whips us into spiritual
Shape. It keeps us actively
Engaged in the necessities of
Life. It allows us to workout
The principles of faith. Prayer
Muscles can carry astounding
Burdens of the heart. Prayer
Exercises bring pressure to
Bear upon adversarial forces
And removes the weight of
The world with a swish of the
Tongue. The inner man
Resemblance that of superman.
Able to leap over high places
In a single bound. Prayer is
Faster than the speed of
Thought. Heaven is calling
You to the ultimate workout,
Prayer.*

PRAY! PRAY! PRAY!

GOOD MORNING WARRIORS!

Prayer is best described as a
One of a kind existence of God.
It places us as spectators in
A galvanized world of scoffers,
Cynics and doubters. But, the
Majesty of prayer is that it
Has converted the likes of
Every challenger daring to
Antagonize our God's reality.
Prayer has arrested the
Hearts of evil men reducing
Them to humble broken men of
Humility and those not willing
To yield to extreme humiliation
Of mind. Prayer is the proof
Of a holy God, central to life
And the mainstay of humanity.

PRAY! PRAY! PRAY!

GOOD MORNING WARRIORS!

Prayer allows the novice as well
As the mature equal access to
The throne room of God. Here the
Mandate and plans are laid out
With precise details and skill
Sets to equip the warriors for
Battle. Prayer is not the
Gathering of warriors with
Thoughtless words heralded by
Traditional mumble jumble. But
Prayer is strategic in nature
Giving definition and rational
Meditation of purpose. It then
Enforces its agenda by invoking
Its rhetoric. It pounds away
Until enemy forces surrenders to
Superior forces of power obtained
From heavens throne room.

PRAY! PRAY! PRAY!

GOOD MORNING WARRIORS!

Morning and evening prayer
Suggests that your life has
Taken on a champions life
Style. The need for pumping
You to pray is obsolete.
Passion and desire has eclipsed
The carnal calls of distractions.
Your now the master of your
Destiny and are a spiritual
Force to be reckon with.
Praying without ceasing is
Your two-edged sword of
Reality, lethal in both the
Heavens and the earth. March
Onward Christian soldiers
Until principalities and thrones
Bow their knees to the
Magnificent name of Jesus.

PRAY! PRAY! PRAY!

GOOD MORNING WARRIORS!

*Prayer released has no
Boundaries or limits. It can
Go anywhere and do anything to
Achieve the impossible. It can
Only be bound by a close mouth.
You were created for strategic
Conversation, to speak purpose-
Fully. Prayer is an invasion
Of words designed to create
Change. God chose prayer as
His tool of communication. He
Created the tongue, the voice
Box, the mouth and the lips to
Produce articulate sounds to
Write his design. You can
Design your life with your
Mouth. Open wide and take
Off the limits.*

PRAY! PRAY! PRAY!

GOOD MORNING WARRIORS!

Prayer are eyes peering into
The supernatural musings of
God. Prayer sees refined
Warriors when blinded by fiery
Trials. Prayer sees concerned
Kingdom citizen when
Indifference placates the church
Conscious. Prayer sees success
When failure grips our focus.
Prayer sees divine health when
Sickness takes residence in
Our bodies. Prayerlessness is
To envision the vast scope of
Hopelessness, for it to has
Eyes to see. But prayer unveils
Hopes expectation. It's
Sight is far reaching, it sees
Beyond the blinding pressures
Of life-giving strength to
Press pass the present barriers.

PRAY! PRAY! PRAY!

GOOD MORNING WARRIORS!

Prayer is a script of victory
Before the battle has been
Fought. Praying finalizes his
Forethoughts. It motivates all
Parties involved, positioning
Them for elevation. Prayer is
A breath of fresh air to all
Who await the process of
Transitioning from carnal
Consequences to faith infused
Faculties. From timid tots to
Tenacious teens and from
Adolescence arrogance to
Agreeable adults. Prayer
Matures the believer step by
Strategic step. God orchestrates
His children's growth spurts
Spiritually. Prayer is lights
Out for immaturity.

PRAY! PRAY! PRAY!

GOOD MORNING WARRIORS!

*Prayer is a 24-hour job, with
Swing shift hours on a seasonal
Basis. We must be flexible,
You can be called upon any
Hour of the day. Your valuable
To the master's plan. He loves
To share his purposes with
Us. God will text his purpose
Upon the hearts of his warriors.
His messages reads like this,
With a big smiley face. Sign
Up at allnightprayer.com or
Noondayprayer.org or
Earlymorningprayer.net. All
Applicants are welcome and
Hiring is on the spot. No
Previous experience necessary,
Just a willing mind and
Humble hearts.*

PRAY! PRAY! PRAY!

GOOD MORNING WARRIORS!

Persistent prayer plus
Repentance brings his presence.
These are the things he desires.
God is always seeking out
The individuals who set high
Standards of excellence on
Their prayer lives. Those who
Do are passionately obsessed
With bringing heaven to earth.
Persistent prayer paves the
Pathway for divine visitation.
It's the only mode of
Transportation capable of
Transporting the glory along
With hosting him while he's
Present. Your prayer life fans
The flames of glory for all
To experience a touch of his
Presence.

PRAY! PRAY! PRAY!

GOOD MORNING WARRIORS!

Prayer is a product of his
Majestic grace. Grace is the
Reason we pray so sincerely for
Others. It's the friend that knocks
At the heart of our friends,
Families and enemies. The grace
To pray fills our hearts with
Compassion for the persecutors
Of our souls. We're never more
Like Jesus then when we allow
Grace to escape our lips. The
Adorning feature of any warrior
Is a heart of grace ready at a
Moment's notice to release it's
Goodness. Grace has never faltered,
Failed or faded away. It is
Still filled to the brim with
Loves enduring embrace. Release
Grace, your full of it, prayer
Makes it an endless reservoir.

PRAY! PRAY! PRAY!

GOOD MORNING WARRIORS!

*Prayer keeps the angelic host
On call day and night. Prayer
Will start conflicts in the
Heavenly realm. Prayer
Warriors understand the rules
Of engagement and will call for
Reinforcements when deemed
Necessary. Prayer postures
Angels as bodyguards, they
Are the invisible secret
Service agents. They guard
Every individual dwelling
In the secret place, they are
The angelic host number one
Assignment. You determine
The level of heavenly activity
That will be involved in your
Life based upon your prayer life.*

PRAY! PRAY! PRAY

GOOD MORNING WARRIORS!

Prayer will keep your life
Balanced and uncomplicated
As possible. Consistent
Prayer will produce its own
Schedule centered around
The life of the spirit.
Prayer will schedule the
Good life, it will manage
Your priorities if you
Have a listening ear. Prayer
Will produce the wisdom of
God in all matters, it will
Make you appear to be a
Genius. Prayer will always
Direct your attention to
His word. Schedule prayer
And prayer will schedule a
Lifetime of supernatural
Victories and successes.

PRAY! PRAY! PRAY!

GOOD MORNING WARRIORS!

*Prayer is the focal point of the
Believer's life. Before we make
Any decisions prayer should
And must be our first priority.
We're required by God to pray
About everything. Prayer is
Designed to remove anxieties
And fears from the dreaded
Decision making processes we
Experience throughout our lives.
God predetermined that the
Decision making process would
Be easy if we would stick to it's
Prerequisites, that is to pray.
Prayer directs us down the
Path towards the right decision.
Peace steps in when prayer is
Offered up, giving you
Clarity of thought and mind.*

PRAY! PRAY! PRAY!

GOOD MORNING WARRIORS!

Warriors are honored for
Their life of bravery and
Sacrifice. Prayer warriors
Are no different. They
Deserve double honor. They
Are the weakest link.
Being weak summons the
Strength of the Almighty.
This makes them invincible,
Being shadowed by God's
 Indestructible power. We
Are more than conquerors
Because of his finish work
 And endless intercession
We stand tall in him, we
Press forward because he's
Been where we're going.
We pray because we want
To imitate his bravery.

PRAY! PRAY! PRAY!

GOOD MORNING WARRIORS!

Prayer charges the dull drab
Life sure to overcome us if
Prayer is lacking. Carnality,
The impostor of the spiritual
Life is exciting to the
Traditionalist, therefore, deceit's
Presence goes undetected.
Prayer will expose the lulling
Agents of progress. Prayer
Uproots the staunchest mindset.
Prayer gnaws away until light
Supersedes the fortresses of
Darkness. Prayer will deliver
Those not willing to fight for
Revelation's light. Love compels
The tireless warriors to pray
Without ceasing to liberate
Our loved ones from adversarial
Hypnotic mind games.

PRAY! PRAY! PRAY!

GOOD MORNING WARRIORS!

*To pray is to see the battle
Through to the end. During
Times of war, the spirit of
God hovers over you, skillfully
Teaching you the intricate
Details of warfare. Prayer is
An exciting journey into the
Unknown realms of God. Prayer
Is for the interested learner
Willing to venture out of a
Life of normalcy. Prayer is a
Investment in time, effort and
Energy. It keeps you edgy and
Aloof from tyrannical assaults.
God is completely enthralled
With your training. He has
Chosen the training grounds,
The times and the various
Enemies to enhance your skills.*

PRAY! PRAY! PRAY!

GOOD MORNING WARRIORS!

The pursuit to developing a
Prayer life starts with a made
Up mind. It will take a tough
Mind to withstand the pressures
Of the carnal arsenals that
Will oppose your mental
Fortitude to pray. Strength
Of will be needed to
Empower the minds resolve.
Discipline and diligence is a
Must if success is to be
Obtained. To be settled in the
Secret place is the goal.
There the reward of presence
Makes the battle and the
Journey a rewarding experience.
And a soldier's story now
Begins to unfold.

PRAY! PRAY! PRAY!